Workbook

Interpersonal relationships

Dr Kimberley O'Brien

HODDER
EDUCATION
AN HACHETTE UK COMPANY

The Publishers would like to thank the following for permission to reproduce copyright material.

Photo credits: **p.2** *l* © Rido /stock.adobe.com, *r* © Monkey Business /stock.adobe.com; **p.3** *l* © Pololia /stock.adobe.com, *r* © Prostock-studio /stock.adobe.com; **p.5** *tl* © Wayhome Studio /stock.adobe.com, *tr* © BullRun /stock.adobe.com, *ml* © Africa Studio /stock.adobe.com, *mr* © Bits and Splits /stock.adobe.com, *bl* © The faces /stock.adobe.com, *br* © Monkey Business /stock.adobe.com; **p.10** © Poulsons Photography /stock.adobe.com; **p.12** © BillionPhotos.com /stock.adobe.com; **p.15** © Javier brosch /stock.adobe.com; **p.18** *ml* © Monkey Business/stock.adobe.com, *bl* © Pixel-Shot/stock.adobe.com; **p.19** *l* © Viacheslav Iakobchuk/stock.adobe.com, *r* © WavebreakMediaMicro/ stock.adobe.com; **p.35** © Wavebreak3/stock.adobe.com; **p.36** *bl* © Per Grunditz/123RF.com, *tr* © Canadian Press/Shutterstock.com; **p.61** *tl* © Wayhome Studio /stock.adobe.com, *tr* © BullRun /stock.adobe.com, *ml* © Africa Studio /stock.adobe.com, *mr* © Bits and Splits /stock.adobe.com, *bl* © The faces /stock.adobe.com, *br* © Monkey Business /stock.adobe.com

l = left; *r* = right; *m* = middle; *t* = top; *b* = bottom

Orders: please contact Bookpoint Ltd, 130 Park Drive, Milton Park, Abingdon, Oxon OX14 4SE. Telephone: +44 (0)1235 827827. Fax: +44 (0)1235 400401. Email education@bookpoint.co.uk Lines are open from 9 a.m. to 5 p.m., Monday to Saturday, with a 24-hour message answering service. You can also order through our website: www.hoddereducation.com

© Dr Kimberley O'Brien 2020

First published in 2020 by
Hodder Education,
An Hachette UK Company
Carmelite House
50 Victoria Embankment
London EC4Y 0DZ
www.hoddereducation.com

Impression number 10 9 8 7 6 5 4 3 2 1

Year   2024 2023 2022 2021 2020

Illustrations by Hannah McCafferey

Typeset in VAG Rounded 14/20pt by DC Graphic Design Limited

Printed in Spain

A catalogue record for this title is available from the British Library.

ISBN: 9781510481633

Contents

Interpersonal relationships

A healthy community is formed with interpersonal relationships, also known as connections between people. Without connections to other humans, most people feel lonely.

Making and keeping friends can be complicated. It takes patience to manage differences and conflicts within any relationship. Interpersonal relationships are like a garden: they need maintenance to help them grow. Regularly dropping in to say 'hello', or checking in by phone, is a good way to communicate with friends, family and other people in your school or neighbourhood. In this way, you can resolve any problems that arise together, which will strengthen the interpersonal relationship.

1 Empathy

Empathy is the skill of being able to understand what someone else is feeling. Empathy is important as it helps you to be a better friend. You may demonstrate your empathy for others through your words, behaviour and actions.

For example, you are showing empathy when you help a friend who is crying by giving them a hug or checking if they are alright. This is because you can understand how they may be feeling.

Empathy is like any other skill: you can improve with practice. Let's work together to build on our skills.

Emotions come in all shapes and sizes. Sometimes, you experience intense emotions. At other times, your emotions can be very mild.

For example:

excited

surprised

thoughtful

sad

angry

unsure

Look at the pictures below.

happy

surprised

angry

sad

scared

anxious

Step 1

Look at the images on page 5 and think about the intensity of each emotion. Is it strong, mild or somewhere in between?

Step 2

Cut out the pictures from pages 59 and 61 and put them in order from mild to strong, using the scale below. Discuss your choices with a partner.

Step 3

Copy the scale below on to a large sheet of paper. Once you are happy with your order for the pictures, paste the pictures on to the scale.

mild (calm)   a bit stronger   quite strong

Can you remember a time when you felt a strong emotion?

Try to describe it below.

_____

_____

_____

_____

_____

_____

_____

Can you remember a time when you felt a mild emotion?

Try to describe it below.

_____

_____

_____

_____

_____

_____

_____

very strong   extreme emotion (rage)

► ACTIVITY ◄ Having the right words

To be empathetic, you often need the right words to express how you feel and to describe how others may be feeling. Let's work on our empathy vocabulary together.

Step 1

Read the sentences below and fill each gap using a word from the box. Try to use your empathy skills to help you choose the right word. Remember, there might be more than one correct answer for each gap.

upset	happy	hurt	worried	embarrassed

frustrated	sad	excited	angry	relieved	nervous

Hussen was walking home when he dropped his ice cream. He was clearly _____ as he was crying.

Ming was jumping and clapping his hands. He was very _____ because he took first prize in the competition.

It was the last rehearsal before the school play. The children were feeling _____ about the opening day.

Jack was going to swimming classes for the first time. He was feeling _____ about using the changing rooms.

8

Step 2

Write a sentence or draw a picture about a time when you felt...

upset

happy

worried

embarrassed

▶ ACTIVITY ◀ Acting empathetic

Looking at your face and body in a mirror can help to tell you how you feel on the inside.

Let's practise mirroring the body language and expressions of another person and trying to understand how they feel.

You will need a partner for this activity.

Step 1

Choose an emotion from the pictures on page 11. Do not tell your partner which one you have chosen.

Step 2

Use your face and body to act out the emotion in the picture.

Step 3

Your partner should copy your expression and how you are using your body. Then they try to guess which picture you have chosen.

Step 4

Did your partner correctly guess which picture you chose? Take turns and count how many you get right.

▶ REFLECTION ◀

How did you get on? Was it easier or harder than you thought it would be?

When do you think it might be difficult to read someone's feelings from their face and body language?

2 Listening to others

Listening is an important skill. By listening, you can learn about other people and the world around you, or follow instructions for things you need to do. Interestingly, the sounds you listen to can affect how you feel and how you behave.

Let's find out more about listening.

▶ ACTIVITY ◀ Recording sounds

Use a recording device, such as a mobile phone or an audio recorder, to capture three sounds from your environment. For example, you could record the sound of voices, music, the wind or rustling paper. Be creative!

For each recording, complete the activity below.

Sound 1

What did you record?

_____

Describe the sound and its characteristics (for example, loud, deep).

_____

_____

_____

_____

How does it make you feel?

_____

_____

How does it make your friend feel?

_____

_____

Do you both feel the same?

_____

_____

Sound 2

What did you record?

_____

Describe the sound and its
characteristics (for example, loud, deep).

_____

_____

_____

How does it make you feel?

_____

_____

How does it make your friend feel?

_____

_____

Do you both feel the same?

_____

_____

Sound 3

What did you record?

_____

Describe the sound and its
characteristics (for example, loud, deep).

_____

_____

_____

How does it make you feel?

_____

_____

How does it make your friend feel?

_____

_____

Do you both feel the same?

_____

_____

When it comes to communication, some people say that listening is much more important than speaking. Everyone likes to be heard.

Sometimes, you listen for fun – for example, when you listen to music or nature or when someone reads to you. At other times, you listen for a specific purpose – for example, when a teacher is telling you what to do next or trying to explain a new idea.

It takes practice to be a good listener, so let's get started.

Step 1

Start to tune into the sounds around you. Maybe you can hear someone whispering or walking towards you, or perhaps you can hear a bird or the wind outside.

Step 2

Close your eyes for a minute or two and relax. (This can be difficult, and you may need to set an alarm or timer.) What do you hear? You might be surprised by how many sounds you notice when your eyes are shut!

Step 3

Open your eyes and describe some of the sounds you heard when your eyes were closed.

_____

_____

_____

_____

Were you surprised by how many sounds you heard? _____

Did you recognize each sound?

_____

Step 4

Choose three sounds and describe how they make you feel.

Sound	How it makes me feel

When someone is talking to you, it is important to be focused and to really consider what they are saying. This is often called active listening .

Active listening is where you tune in to what someone else is saying by engaging in the conversation. You ask questions, repeat what you hear and offer support and understanding for the other person's point of view.

Let's practise. Work with a friend or a parent for this activity.

Step 1

Choose two special dishes or foods that you would take with you to a desert island. Draw and describe them in the space below.

Ask your partner to do the same.

Step 2

Take turns to describe your dishes to each other. Do not say the name of the dish!

Think about these questions:

- Why did you choose each dish?

- What is so good about it?

- How is it made?

- How does it make you feel when you eat it?

Step 3

After your partner has finished speaking, write as many details as possible about their two favourite dishes.

The number of details you can remember shows how carefully you were listening and paying attention.

3 Working in groups and teams

Humans often organize themselves in groups. For example, your family, your circle of friends, your class, your sports team, and even the children on your street – they are all groups!

Make a list of the groups you belong to.

Groups work well when group members:

- cooperate
- communicate with respect
- take responsibility for their actions
- compromise.

Let's find out how well you work in a group.

► ACTIVITY ◄ Cooperation quiz

Answer the following questions.

1	I often take time to consider my friends' ideas.	Yes	No
2	I offer support to friends when they need my help in class.	Yes	No
3	I let people go in front of me when we're waiting in line.	Yes	No
4	I like to listen to everyone's ideas before starting a group activity.	Yes	No
5	I am happy for someone else to lead.	Yes	No
6	I prefer to take turns rather than go first all the time.	Yes	No
7	I like group work.	Yes	No
8	I like to share my things.	Yes	No
9	I work faster when I'm on a team.	Yes	No
10	I like to discuss things with other people.	Yes	No

Results

Count up your 'Yes' answers.

1–4	5–7	8–10
Wow! You like to work alone. Working in a group takes patience and practice. It also gives you access to more skills and ideas.	You are a good team player, but you also value time alone. Most people do! Group work takes practice – it gets easier over time.	You are a Teamwork Whizz! Well done. You have demonstrated fantastic cooperation skills and are a great team player.

Being respectful is a really important skill when you are working in a group. You can show respect in many ways, including:

- speaking kindly
- listening
- waiting your turn
- cleaning up your mess
- behaving appropriately (for example, being quiet in a library)
- arriving on time.

Let's help Jessie improve her group work skills.

Read the story about Jessie's day and then answer the questions.

6.30am

Jessie's mum knocks on the bedroom door to tell Jessie the alarm has gone off and it is time to get dressed.

Jessie is tired. She makes a sound like 'aargh' before throwing her pillow at the wall.

Was Jessie respectful?   Yes   No

Explain why or how.

_____

_____

_____

What could Jessie do differently next time?

_____

_____

_____

6.45am

Jessie finally gets out of bed and gets dressed for school.

Then she helps her little sister Amy by tying her shoelaces for her.

Was Jessie respectful?   Yes   No

Explain why or how.

_____

_____

_____

What could Jessie do differently next time?

_____

_____

_____

7.30am

Jessie and Amy leave for school. Jessie's mum realizes that Jessie has left her lunch at home and runs down the street to give it to her.

Jessie puts her lunch in her bag but forgets to say thank you to her mum.

Was Jessie respectful?   Yes   No

Explain why or how.

_____

_____

_____

What could Jessie do differently next time?

_____

_____

_____

7.45am

Jessie and Amy arrive at Amy's preschool. Amy's friend Jo stops Jessie to tell her a long story about her pet fish. Jessie listens carefully and asks lots of questions, and this makes Jo really happy.

Jessie remembers to help Amy put her bag away. She says goodbye to Amy before she leaves.

Was Jessie respectful?   Yes   No

Explain why or how.

_____

_____

_____

What could Jessie do differently next time?

_____

_____

_____

9.00am

Jessie's friend Billy is late for class and, as he runs in, he knocks a tin of pencils off the teacher's desk. Jessie helps him to pick up the pencils before the teacher arrives.

In maths, a boy calls Mr Chew 'Mr Chew Chew Train' and the whole class laughs.

Was Jessie respectful?   Yes   No

Explain why or how.

_____

_____

_____

_____

_____

_____

What could Jessie do differently next time?

_____

_____

_____

_____

_____

_____

_____

Lunchtime

Jessie plays with her friends Billy and Ruby. They take turns shooting hoops at the basketball court.

Andy arrives and asks if he can join in. The others decide that, since they now have an even number of people, they can play two-against-two basketball.

Was Jessie respectful?　　　　　　　　　　Yes　No

Explain why or how.

_____

_____

_____

What could Jessie do differently next time?

_____

_____

_____

Being cooperative and solving problems

When groups work together to solve a challenge, they share ideas and suggestions about what to do. Often, group members will have to accept someone else's idea to solve the challenge. This process may require a lot of **compromises**.

Compromising makes it possible for groups or individuals to find a good outcome to a dilemma or challenge. You have probably been compromising all your life without realizing it – for example, by taking turns in the classroom, or by agreeing to play football with your brother if he will play Lego with you afterwards.

Compromising involves:

- **trust** – you need to trust that everyone will be fair
- understanding – you must understand that different things are important or valuable to different people
- **flexibility** – you must be open and willing to try different solutions.

Compromise is important, because people have different values. Let's see how compromising works.

Use the checkboxes below to rate how important these things are to you:

	Very important		Quite important		Not important		Totally unimportant	
	Me	Friend	Me	Friend	Me	Friend	Me	Friend
Eating a healthy breakfast								
Staying up late								
Reading								
Choosing my own clothes								
Watching TV								

Then ask a friend to do the same.

Compare your checkboxes. Do you value the same things? How are you different?

_____

_____

_____

_____

_____

_____

_____

_____

Now let's try to find solutions to the following challenges. Remember to consider everyone's ideas.

Question 1

Your school is organizing a fundraising event. They need ideas about products to sell. Jessica, Hussein and Annelise need to agree on the best way forward.

- Jessica wants a flower stall.

- Hussein wants a toy stall.

- Annelise wants a jewellery stall.

Suggest a way they could compromise.

_____

_____

_____

Question 2

Your brother wants to have some friends to sleep over but you have already made plans to have a party. How can you agree on the best way forward?

Suggest a way that you and your brother could compromise.

_____

_____

_____

4 Helping others to succeed

Once in a while, you might spot a chance to help someone. These opportunities are special and you should take them! Why? Because helping others to succeed will make you feel good about yourself.

Imagine you see a boy trying to remove his kite from a tree. He is pulling the string but it will not budge. Quickly, you reach up and start shaking a branch. The boy smiles – you are on the same team now. When the kite falls to the ground, you share the success!

It is a proven fact that helping other people gives us a sense of purpose and makes us feel good. It can also help us to make new friends. When we care about the same thing, this brings us closer together and often makes us try harder to succeed.

You can contribute in lots of ways. Some people love the spotlight, while others prefer to be quiet achievers. Regardless of your role, you can always contribute to the outcome.

Let's see how you like to contribute.

Step 1

Read the list of roles and definitions below.

Presenter	You like to be in front of an audience.
Measurer	You like to obtain data and know the facts.
Organizer	You can see the big picture and how to achieve it.
Designer	You are creative and enjoy working with colours.
Deep thinker	You absorb information and make sense of it.
Monitor	You like to observe and take in the details.
Scribe	You can put things into words and love to write.
Judge	You consider all the options and make an informed decision.
Assistant	You are happy to support anyone who needs help.
Listener	You know the importance of understanding everyone's point of view.

Choose three roles you feel represent your style of contribution. Give an example for each role.

Role	Example
Listener	I often pay attention to instructions, so I can help my friends later.

How do others like to contribute?

Let's complete a survey.

Step 1

With your teacher's help, ask five of your friends to complete the survey below.

Thank you for participating in this contribution survey about what you do in your classroom.

Please answer the following questions by circling Yes or No.

1	I help others by encouraging them when they need it.	Yes	No
2	I help others by keeping our classroom tidy.	Yes	No
3	I help others by taking turns.	Yes	No
4	If I have an idea, I will share it with my class.	Yes	No
5	I like to be given jobs in class.	Yes	No

Step 2

Count how many people answered 'Yes' to each question.

Now record the findings from your survey on the graph below.

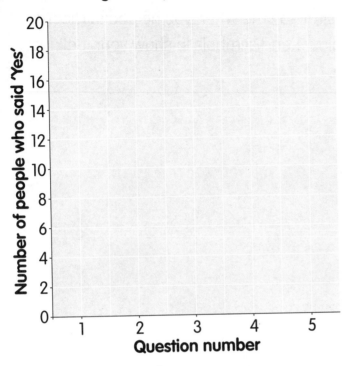

Step 3

Which ways of contributing were most common? Which ways of contributing were least common? Why do you think this is?

_____
_____
_____
_____

Step 4

Think about the different ways people like to contribute in your class. Some people may be great listeners, while others like to present or measure outcomes.

There are many things people can do to make your classroom a better place by doing the things they love. Can you think of three?

1 _____
_____

2 _____
_____

3 _____
_____

▶ REFLECTION ◀

How do you feel when you do something to help someone else succeed?

Draw a picture to illustrate a time when you helped someone else succeed. Use colours and symbols to show your feelings about this experience.

5 Advocating for rights and needs

Did you know, advocating for your own needs is very important?

To **advocate** for yourself means to represent yourself, to make sure your opinion is heard. You can also advocate for another person, or for a cause.

To advocate for your own rights and needs, you need the right tools, support and confidence. You might find it easier to express yourself at home rather than at school, or with one friend rather than in front of a whole group.

With practice, you can become better at representing yourself.

Have you heard of these inspiring advocates?

This is Malala Yousafzai from Pakistan. She believed everyone should be allowed an education, so she challenged a rule that said girls could not go to school. She went to school every day, even though she was not allowed.

One day, when she was 15 years old, she was shot at while she was on a school bus with friends. Luckily, she survived and continues to speak out and advocate the importance of education for all.

She published her first book, *I Am Malala*, at the age of 16. In 2014, when she was just 17, she became the youngest person to win the Nobel Peace Prize.

This is Greta Thunberg from Sweden. She is a teenage climate activist. She believes in protecting the planet and fighting climate change.

At the age of 16, she started skipping school on Fridays and going on strike instead. She protested outside the government offices and held up a handwritten poster saying 'School strike for climate'. Her actions have spread and now, millions of young people all over the world have organized similar protests.

When Greta is asked to speak at meetings all over the world, she tries to find ways to travel that do not damage the environment. She spent two weeks sailing across the Atlantic on a zero-emissions yacht to speak at the UN Climate Action Summit in New York City!

Here are some ways you can advocate for your rights and needs:

- Writing a letter
- Making a sign
- Researching your rights
- Preparing a speech
- Scheduling a meeting with a decision maker
- Finding a support person, group or organization
- Creating a petition
- Protesting

Let's practise with two of these tools.

Action 1: Letter writing

Imagine your school has banned ball games. Everyone is upset and unsure what to do. You decide to advocate for your rights by writing a letter to your school principal. In your letter, you will explain the impact of the ban on yourself and the other students at your school.

Write your name and class here.

Write the name of
your Principal here.

Write the name
and address of
your school here.

Write today's
date here.

Write your school
principal's name here.

Dear

Start the letter
by saying
what you are
unhappy about.

What do you
want? Suggest
some solutions.

Sign off your
letter like this.
Write your name
in the space.

Yours sincerely,

To advocate for your rights successfully, you need to understand other people's perspectives. You can better understand other points of view by creating opportunities for  . If you engage in a dialogue, you have a conversation or a discussion: you listen and acknowledge other people's points of view.

Let's practise advocating for our own rights while also understanding other points of view.

▶ **ACTIVITY** ◀ **Can you understand someone else's perspective?**

Look at the opposing images below and try to describe the different perspectives.

Can you explain each person's perspective?

_____

_____

_____

_____

_____

Can you explain each person's perspective?

_____

_____

_____

_____

_____

Can you explain each person's perspective?

_____

_____

_____

_____

_____

Your town has introduced a new rule that forbids children to ride bikes or skateboards in public parks. Some residents have complained about the noise and safety concerns. You decide to work with your friends to advocate for your rights.

You want to schedule a meeting with the local mayor, so you can try to understand his perspective and find a compromise.

To ensure you are well prepared, you will need to work through these steps. First, number the steps in the correct order.

☐ A Have a meeting and conversation.

☐ B Find the postal or email address for the mayor's office.

☐ C Draft a list of questions.

☐ D Find the mayor's name.

☐ E Send the mayor a letter or email to arrange a meeting.

What questions would you ask the mayor?

_____

_____

_____

_____

_____

How could you show the mayor that you are prepared to compromise? Choose two of the options below to show you understand the mayor's perspective.

1 Children are only allowed to ride bikes or skateboards before and after school. ☐

2 Children are only allowed to ride bikes or skateboards in designated areas. ☐

3 Children must dismount around crossings. ☐

4 Children must look out for elderly people. ☐

5 Children must keep noise to a minimum. ☐

▶ ACTIVITY ◀ Making a sign

In groups of four, create a sign to say why children should be allowed to ride bikes and skateboards in public parks.

6 Making decisions

You make decisions all the time. Some decisions are easy to make, while others are quite difficult. Sometimes you have to choose between two equally good things, such as riding your bike or riding your scooter. At other times, you have to choose between two things you do not want to do, such as setting the table or hanging out the washing!

Let's practise decision-making.

▶ ACTIVITY ◀ Making simple and hard decisions

Did you know, a child makes approximately 3,000 choices and decisions every day? Let's think about these daily decisions and rate them according to how easy or hard they are to make.

Step 1

Read about the decisions below. Think about how easy or hard it would be to choose between the options.

Write the letter on the decide-o-meter to show how easy or difficult it would be to make the decision.

The decide-o-meter

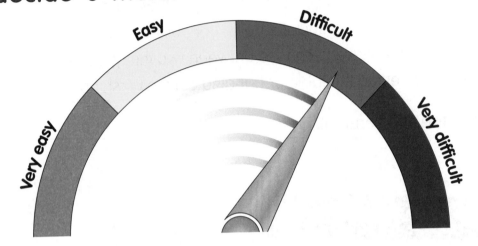

Decide between the options.

A   Write a story or draw a picture.

B   Eat an ice cream or eat an apple.

C   Get extra TV time or choose something yummy for dinner.

D   Play your favourite board game or learn a new game.

E   Watch a new movie or have a friend over to play.

F   Sleep over at a friend's house or have extra computer time.

Step 2

When you have put all the decisions on the decide-o-meter, compare your answers with a friend. You could also ask someone at home to complete the decide-o-meter.

Discuss how you made your decisions.

As you know, you make many decisions every day. Some decisions are almost automatic – you do not even think about them. Yet there are many other decisions you need to think about more carefully.

Let's explore your decision-making further.

Small decisions

Look at these examples. Then write about or draw a similar small decision that you make almost every day.

Example	Your turn
Richard decides between cereal or toast for breakfast every day.	
Sarah decides between wearing her hair in a ponytail or wearing her hair down.	

Not so easy decisions

Look at these examples. Then write about or draw a similar, more complex decision that you make almost every day.

Example	Your turn
Ali had to choose a chapter in a book to read and present to the class.	
John is considering whether to invite the whole class to his birthday party or only a few friends.	

Hard decisions

Look at this example. Then write about or draw a similar complex decision you might need to make.

Example	Your turn
Lucy has to decide what to buy for her big sister's birthday.	

Sometimes, you have to make big decisions, like choosing between two things you love equally. At other times, you make decisions that come with a lot of responsibility and stay with you for a long time, such as buying a pet.

When you have to make a big decision, it is important to think ahead and consider a range of factors. You can use these three simple steps.

Making big decisions

1 Collect: Gather information.

- What information do you need?

- Who can you ask for help?

- Where can you look for information and find more facts or experiences?

2 Check: Think about the pros and cons of your decision.

- What are the positive points?

- What are the negative points?

3 Consider: Think about any consequences of your decision.

- Who will your decision affect?

- How will the decision make you feel?

You can use the decision journey template on the next page to help you make big decisions. Every step along the path will bring you closer to reaching your decision.

Step 1

Think about a big decision you need to make. Write it here.

_____

_____

_____

_____

Step 2

Look at each stop in turn and answer the questions.

▶ REFLECTION ◀

Do you feel more prepared to make a decision now? What was helpful and what was difficult? What would you do differently next time, if anything?

The decision journey

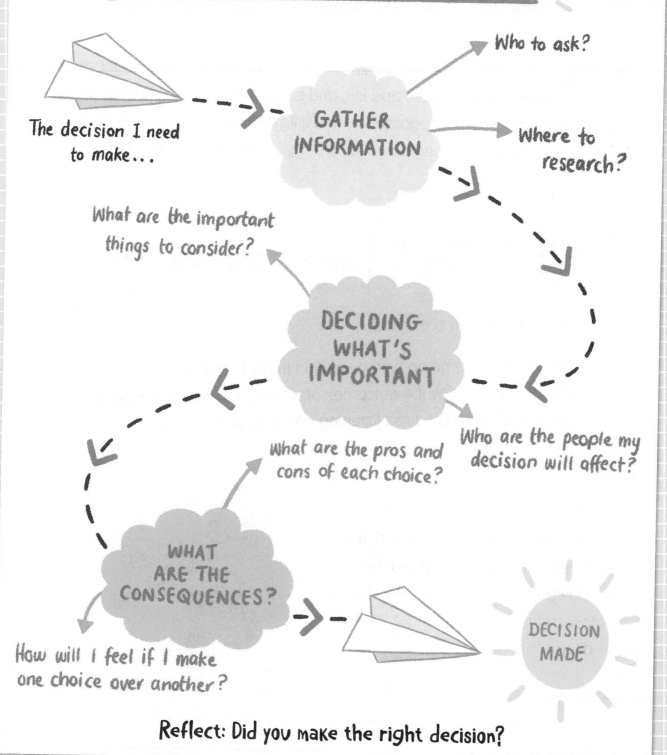

DECISION JOURNEY

The decision I need to make...

GATHER INFORMATION

Who to ask?

Where to research?

What are the important things to consider?

DECIDING WHAT'S IMPORTANT

Who are the people my decision will affect?

What are the pros and cons of each choice?

WHAT ARE THE CONSEQUENCES?

How will I feel if I make one choice over another?

DECISION MADE

Reflect: Did you make the right decision?

7 Negotiation

Negotiation is about working together to find a solution that works for everyone. It involves listening, being patient and fair, and being willing to compromise or meet halfway. This means being prepared to win a little and lose a little. The goal of negotiation is to find 'common ground' or 'the right balance' to move forward.

Let's practise.

► ACTIVITY ◄ Review the scenarios

Read the following scenarios.

Once you have come up with a solution to each problem, work with a partner to role-play the outcomes of your negotiation. Remember to be flexible and use good listening and compromising skills.

Scenario 1

Tom has a new drone and his friend, Ben, really wants to try it. Tom's worried the drone may get stuck up a tree if Ben has a turn. How can the two boys find a solution to this dilemma?

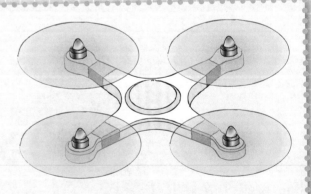

_____

_____

_____

_____

_____

Scenario 2

Kate wants to sleep in her treehouse with her friend, Millie. All the parents say it will be too cold. What could the girls suggest to their parents that might fix the problem?

_____

_____

_____

_____

Scenario 3

Sarah and her twin brother, Sam, are allowed to go to the cinema but they cannot agree on what to watch. Their parents want them to go to the same movie. How could they solve this dilemma?

_____

_____

_____

_____

_____

▶ REFLECTION ◀

How did you get on? Which skills did you use? Which skills do you think you need to work on?

_____

_____

_____

It is quite common to disagree when you are negotiating with someone, especially if you know the other person well. But focusing on your differences can get in the way of finding a solution: if you refuse to consider other options, you will both end up feeling frustrated.

It is better to look for things you can agree on. This is called **finding common ground** and it is the best way to find a way forward when there are differences of opinion.

Here is your chance to practise!

Read the following scenarios and help the characters to find common ground.

Scenario 1

Olivia and Benjamin want to raise money to protect the orangutans in Malaysia.

- Olivia wants to make and sell scented candles. She plans to use orange peel in the candle wax to create a sweet orange smell.

- Benjamin decides he would like to sell orange juice. He plans to squeeze the oranges Olivia has peeled.

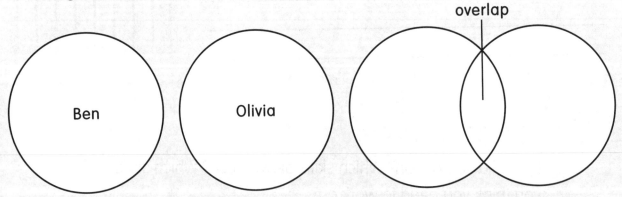

Question: How much do Olivia and Benjamin's ideas overlap? If they are the same, the circles will cover each other. If they are very different, the overlap will be small.

In the box below, draw two circles to represent Benjamin and Olivia's ideas. Overlap the circles to show how much their ideas overlap.

How much common ground do Olivia and Benjamin have?

_____

_____

Scenario 2

Harlo and Cairo cannot agree on anything. Harlo wants to play with her kite, but Cairo wants to use the sticks from the kite to make a fire. He plans to use the kite string to get the first flames started. Harlo will not let Cairo touch her kite: now that she knows his plan, she will not let it out of her sight!

Question: How much do Harlo and Cairo's ideas overlap?

In the box below, draw two circles to represent Harlo and Cairo's ideas. Overlap the circles to show how much their ideas overlap in Scenario 2.

How much common ground do Harlo and Cairo have?

_____

_____

Negotiating is fun. You can use humour, learn new things about someone and make your relationship stronger.

Let's help Alex, Emily and their mum find the right balance as they try to resolve some challenges.

Comic 1

Emily and Alex are brother and sister. They are trying to agree on what to do after school. Emily wants to go to the park and join her team for an important game of soccer. Alex wants to ride his bike at a local track with his friends.	Here's the challenge. They need to stay together and they can only go out after doing their jobs at home. Emily has to tidy her bedroom and Alex needs to water the vegetable garden.

Now it is your turn.

In the blank comic strips on page 55, suggest two solutions to the problem. Use humour, good listening, flexibility and compromising skills. Add speech bubbles or thought bubbles if you like!

Speech bubbles are used for words that are spoken out loud.

Thought bubbles are used to show inner thoughts and feelings.

Solution 1

Before	During	After

Solution 2

Before	During	After

Show your answers to a friend, teacher or parent. Which solution do they prefer: Solution 1 or Solution 2?

Ask what they liked about their preferred solution.

Comic 2

Amira and Aisha are sisters. They are allowed to decide what their family will do at the weekend.

Amira loves rock climbing and Aisha loves the beach.

Here's the challenge.

They need to consider that their mother is scared of heights and their father is not a strong swimmer.

What activities will make the day fun for the whole family, including themselves?

Now it is your turn.

In the blank comic strips on page 57, suggest two solutions to the problem. Use humour, good listening, flexibility and compromising skills. Add speech bubbles or thought bubbles if you like!

Solution 1

Before	During	After

Solution 2

Before	During	After

Show your answers to a friend, teacher or parent.
Which solution do they prefer: Solution 1 or Solution 2?

Ask what they liked about their preferred solution.

Glossary

Active listening
Tuning in to what someone else is saying by nodding, using eye contact and asking questions. You may agree, disagree, offer your support and ask questions to be sure you fully understand.

Advocate
To represent yourself, another person, or a cause, by making sure a different opinion or experience is heard and appreciated.

Compromise
Finding solutions which make it possible for people to find common ground.

Consequences
The effects or impacts of a decision or action.

Dialogue
To have a conversation or discussion, listening and acknowledging other people's points of view.

Empathy
Being able to appreciate what someone else is feeling, by imagining how you would feel in their position.

Finding common ground
Looking for things you can agree on.

Flexibility
Being open and willing to try different solutions.

Interpersonal relationships
Connections between people.

Negotiation
The process of working together to find a solution everyone can agree on.

Pros and cons
Positive and negative impacts of something; advantages and disadvantages.

Understanding
Recognising that different things are important or valuable to different people.

Trust
Believing in the honesty and reliability of others.

Templates

Cards for Activity on pages 4–5

Cut out the different emotions. ✂

excited

surprised

thoughtful

sad

angry

unsure

Cut out the photos.